Red Nest

Red

Nest

Gillian Jerome

Nightwood Editions

Nightwood Editions
Box 1779
Gibsons, BC Canada V0N 1V0

The book has been produced on 100% post-consumer recycled, ancient-forest-free paper, processed chlorine-free and printed with vegetable-based dyes.

Cover by Brad Cran
Cover art by Judith Scott, courtesy of Creative Growth Art Center, Oakland, California

Nightwood Editions acknowledges financial support of its publishing program from the Canada Council for the Arts and the Book Publishing Industry Development Program (BPIDP), and from the British Columbia Arts Council.

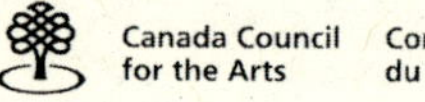

LIBRARY AND ARCHIVES CANADA CATALOGUING IN PUBLICATION

Jerome, Gillian
Red nest / Gillian Jerome.

Poems.
ISBN 978-0-88971-241-6

I. Title.

PS8619.E76R43 2009 C811'.6 C2009-903155-8

For Patricia Alice Donovan Brady
& Marjorie Ann Dillon Jerome,
two great dames.

Already now the night is nigh;
From distant chimneys, there, the smoke
Is curling up; and, see, the oak
Throws lengthening shadows from the hills
The spreading gloom the valley fills.

– Virgil

Contents

One

Tenement Song 13
Evolution 16
Neighbourhood 17

Two

Apiary of Underclothes 31
Unknown Girl from Bountiful 32
Natura Domestica 33
Black Swans 34
They Lived in a Shack on Brunel Street 36
Midsummer 37
Birds Fly High Here, 38
Colonic 39
Revelations 40
Pound of Water, Piece of Bread 41
Constellation 42

Three

To the hills and the mountains under sky 47
Epilogue 62

Four

Firstborn 65
Midwinter 66
Flood 67
Evacuation Procedures 68
Red 70
The Looking Glass 79
Starry Heavens 80
Twilight 81

Notes and Acknowledgements 83

One

Tenement Song

Sing the song of centuries
Sing the song of ninety-degree summers
The song of syphilis
The song of electrical storms inside us

Sing the song of seagulls
Sing the song of doors slammed
The song of bosoms in our shirts
The song of drunken parrots

Sing the song of cauldrons bubbling
The song of our daughters filing past
The song of school kids revving their engines
Sing the low song of wolves sharpening their teeth

Sing the song of the living
Sing the song of mail in their hands
Of marbles, keys, envelopes sliced open
The song of shoes shuffling past

Sing the song of sneezing and coughing and changing direction
Sing the song of Theseus' madness, midsummer
The song of hard-working, of happenstance
                                        of some tinker's reliquary
The song of tsunamis

Sing the song of pigeons scoring the wind
Sing the song of obstacles, of evergreens
The song of our liturgy, the song of the answering machine
The song of the alcove, the lean-to
                                        the chlorophyll bright in the trees

Sing the song of Apollo, of Agamemnon
The song of Cassandra, the loneliest woman in the world
The song of the swan gliding in swamp water
The song of the clavicle, the cave dweller

Sing the song of our small breastedness, our bordellos
Sing the song of our nightgowns, our decrepit teeth
The song of our hips, our split feet
The song of our thirty-three sails in thirty-three un-
                                        sailable waters

Sing the song of Cecil nailing the shingles to the roof

Sing the song of mist hovering in the button trees

of Caesarean sunset

The song of hydro bills, of snowstorms

The song of bottles, of algae, of billy goats

Sing the song of Mars, of Mercury, of the Americas

The song of our finger bones tapping the locks

The song of the pale bow of the moon, the sun

Slipping into our song:

Dear Landlord,

Evolution

Fat notes from the church Wurlitzer
kill a clump of flies.

We chuck stones at the rows
of one-eyed blackbirds.

When the sun beckons, we slouch pale and bright-eyed toward it.

Heavy lids of the Blessed Virgins
flutter at us from every passing yard.

We charge down Pigweed Hill.
Snap the heads off dandelions.

Cool nights, we watch
the neighbours fight
inside their kitchens.

Each year some fool gets caught in the pines—

Neighbourhood

Beyond the streetlamps
and hands of oak trees

Dogs sift quietly by their owners
into the dream life of dogs

The lake is a swamp
of syringes and cars

Crows occupy
hydro lines

muttering at each other
to and fro

Mothers pluck their babes
from the lake

Carry them over their shoulders
home

The stones roll out of alignment
stones of dandelions and cigarettes

stones of cursing and fouling out
stones of leaning into a kiss and missing

Swings without people in them
rock back and forth

If it weren't for the ponies

wetting their noses
in the clover

radiant violet

in love with buttercups
and Dalmatians

there'd be no mess of torsos
asleep under the sun

The traffic sign out yonder traps the iris
The traffic sign says, *Slow down*

Particles of sand
wait in splendour

for the sound of thunder
for the sound of rain—

sacks of marbles dropping
on corrugated iron—

How shall we greet each other,
come twilight, come the treacle of stars?

Blackbird hanging from the elm tree
so red-winged and bodacious

So much more beautiful than the road

Old ladies in lawn chairs
bathe their ankles in swamp water

Sip vodka through straws

Pink-yellow-blue light
dances off their sunglasses

They fall asleep with Twinkie
bits on their chins

Their feet commingling
with the feet of trees

The trees make a ravine

Make a maze of planets
for kids to disappear in

Kids pick burrs
off each other

'til the sun tinkles out
and sinks

Rats carry their groceries
one by one

Mother pushes her kid
in a shopping cart

Consider this day
this daily admonition

"If you want one, you'll find one,
put your faith in that"

There is a point at which
nobody uses lights

Bonfires cook cobs of corn
Bake your eyeballs, your elbows

Consider your beginnings as reverie
wrapped in aluminum foil

Kids run through stalks of wheat
'til 10 o'clock

That fellow in the jean jacket
collects carburetors

Kids dangle from the jungle gym
calling "Mom,"   "Mom,"

to the all-night restaurant
Love is nocturnal, so is hope

Sign us all up for sewing lessons
and we'll sew

That screech, is that a band saw or Satan
sharpening his wings?

Counsellor   tiler   janitor
teacher   plumber

Retirees and a dealer
who lives in his parents' basement

Believe it or not we all
rake our lawns

Kids draw
their dreams out in chalk

Blow the hairdos
off dandelions

"You take the hand you get dealt"
Even the concrete statue

of the shepherd boy
Even his erection

Tremors in the birch trees
speed things up and

slow things
'til we're whole again

In good weather
we squeeze the creature

to get our trash out on time

Accept the whole mind—
even Gordie, the lame guy

who chucks bottles of Tanqueray
into the hedge

"Somebody help him, he's lost his pants"
The ambulance is here again

It seems like every winter
we're a few pounds over

We dye our heads chestnut
to confuse the squirrels

Bills pile up
on our kitchen counters

We'd like to go away
each year to Mexico—

for the hot pink umbrellas
in the soda

for the swim-up bar
and the oiled gods

wearing Speedos—
But we don't

We sit by the fire spearing wieners
The kids run in pairs double-legged and afraid

Cars roar past and we cuss at them
We spin vinyl in Tony's garage to remember

what it was like   At night, we live in our kitchens
Crush garlic cloves and rub them into the pork

When the grass browns we unfasten
each other's sprinklers

Steal each other's two-by-fours

Sundays we sit on our porches
talking on the cordless…

Really, we should invest in a vineyard
somewhere in the Interior

All day the slide winks at the sun
We punch in and punch out

Someone else takes care of our kids
'til we haul them home and feed them

These here are posies   This one's lady's slipper
These speeds won't be solved by speed bumps

We watch dragons float by us on the lake water
The needles and pink condoms

The mass immigration of dogs
Someone's got to reconcile our existence

with all these potted geraniums
How utopian—the sprinkler—

Lacunae will return in blossoms
In time capsules the kids bury

for the dogs to dig up—
In terra-cotta flower pots

broken on the front steps
This oath has been written out in Lik-M-Aid

for all the coyotes and bedraggled dogs
We anchor the sidewalks, ears cocked—

"At the end of the day
When it's time to go

We go alone

We go without shoes on
Irrigated by blood"

T w o

Apiary of Underclothes

After the beer parlour, we set off for the islands
drinking whiskey from Tupperware cups. We jimmied
the radio for baseball—Expos were up.
I didn't know what day it was, or the year.
Finally, I thought, a good-sized man, and held the wheel.
Strands of silence floated up between us
like duck shit in the lake water. It happened
right when the days held 'til ten o'clock. Fireflies. June bugs.
Every few miles we stuck our heads into the slipstream
to whet our eyeballs. Both of us taken
with the lights flickering on the dash. We felt
ghosts hovering over the scab of last year's abominable fires.
Have you heard so-and-so's having a baby? Well no.
Well yes. I hummed my favorite Bo Diddleys,
rattled off some names of local birds. Jays
scooped it finally. When the car stopped
furs of dandelions flew around us
& we hastened like they did
into that broom.

Unknown Girl from Bountiful

Midwife stares at my privates like a clock.
Across from me the whole time
my seven sister wives sit in their seven
sagging underpants & prairie dresses.
There go the crows again throwing tantrums.
All the world's a bed of bowel movements & blood.
My eyes lock to the wall's tiles. A pop bottle drops from its crate.
We're on all fours under the Skimmerhorns, broken only
by the garden's trowelled rows. Mother's yelling *Dinnertime!*
through a rolled-up newspaper. Crows thread their wreaths of Kleenex.
Above us, they scoop & freefall, fishing in eavestroughs for worms
& wads of bread. Can't shake 'em: heavy wings hover at my shoulders—
their eyestrings yank at every bone! The room
slides & stitches. It stones & quiets down.
You better push hard, the baby's heart… & my head's
a ladder of tinny bells. The midwife's hand pulls
my privates like fruit leather over some mewling
skull. Guided by the earth's esophagus, some shiny
lure, some duckling dunked in flotsam: out, out
the smell of wire fence & apples wrinkled with rot.

Natura Domestica

Dragonflies flicker in & out of the sun
wearing helmets & buzzing full throttle
while flies bat around the hog scraps I left
at breakfast. There's catharsis in this habit
of bleaching the grout between the tiles—
I spend my days hunkering around the house
looking like the pregnant male seahorse
minutes before he spits out his young. Tonight
we'll have spaghetti & beer & I'll feel a little more
Lauren Bacall—will you call me then?
The seahorse has sex organs
any man would be proud of—no
Rocky Balboa, mind you, but he fits.
Roll out the rubber: Every ounce is needed to mobilize our forces!
What's the destiny of these weighty bones
wrapped in a terry cloth robe? You know,
the cow's belly, udders & teats should be wiped off
with a damp cloth before milking. Mother
used to tell me this before dates. Every day
I build sculptures of stones for the garden,
night after night the raccoons plow 'em
down. What are they getting even for?
Mister, you should move closer—
when the sun sinks & the breeze cools things,
you can see the catfish mingling, their organs
shining for us in the dark.

Black Swans

I.

You can't watch yourself wanting water,
can't stand the urge to drink & so
you go for days so thirsty it hurts me.
Upon the tablets of water is written in code
all your self doesn't want itself to know.
We're in no condition for alms or driving
or fucking like mad dogs in the backseat—
but my solemn wish is that we could be.
Will you blaze with me? Will you fall down
the rabbit hole crushed against me & call up
cups of us flushed & motionless?
For days now my guts have been busted.
How to be sick with someone else's grief?
I must tell you, sweetheart, I've thought of us
trespassing the dark corners of the drive-in
to share a burger platter—

II.

Vowels trap me. My tongue can't fathom anything
but *o*. Oleanders fall into my arms & we recite genesis
by passing tiny silver fish mouth to mouth.
Genesis is a moon over New York City
& we're skating on ice in Central Park.
For this you'll win my heart, my dear Lord of Things Untoward.
Meanwhile, power cables fall short of breath
& streetlights weaken at the knees. Take this jar
I've filled for you, a gift of my four extracted teeth.
Their roots resemble the tendrils of lilies
& smell like someone's timely death.
From far off, fate careens toward us
with its souped-up engines & filaments of stars.
Can you hear the band playing their cellos
for us? All the belladonnas taut as strings.
In my dream bulls gather. Roses grow out of my eyes.
The bulls clot the street. See them run. See me running
toward them.

They Lived in a Shack on Brunel Street

We roamed   we ate   we slung the lard
in silence   silence was a gold coin in the eye
silence was buttercups woven into my hair
so words couldn't hurt me
the counters stank of bottles of milk gone bad
the air in the kitchen was thick with grease
Aunty couldn't clean a thing—she spread
our clothes still soaked in blood
face up on the guck
where the dogs played
when I shuffled past the neighbours' houses I prayed
Lord Jesus Almighty Make Me Invisible—Hear Ye—
for years that prayer stuck by me
the dogs growled about their leeches
the floorboards stank of sour laundry
at midnight we waltzed in sock feet
to & fro around the radio & all we imagined
that glamorous life   when I went to bed I dreamt
I poured a placenta into a vase & drank it

Midsummer

Out at Trout Lake the kids are splayed in the umbra of the sun
feeding goldfish with plankton. There's a glut
as it happens, along the coast so the fish are smallish

and demented. But parrots have been welcomed
into the noses, ears, armpits, hearts of the children
where they never hasten to repeat

the dirty words they teach them. Nobody hears
their curses but me and so I say them softly back to myself—
Fuckhead. Shitballs. Gaylord.

The sun is a soothsayer with a parched tongue
and lips the colour of iron. Under the Tattletree
I try to glean my thoughts from myself

wondering with all these children at my feet
where the peace went and what it wants to say
to the rank-and-file creatures out for a stroll, of the tamed pigeons breeding

above me in the dovecote. So remote is the island
of myself from my self, even the circuitous circus
of the heart has found in the grass

slumber to shut itself up.

Birds Fly High Here,

sun reclines for a rest. Tell me
what you want to do about this new soul,
this bird of a girl beating her wings under downy blankets
while winter drops
all over us, our roof, our trellis, our clothesline
& the crows plunge into the white
canvas of the world. My heart
hides out here in the thickets of blankets
as vulnerable to breaking as ice.

Glass goblets. Glass globes
hang from the ceilings of sleep.

Shrubs cover up;
the roses are coated in frost; people
leave bootstamps in the sidewalks.
What is it that makes us small &, without
reliable weather & clean water, invariably
lonely? Tires scrawl black *s*
shapes down the street, something
like a mirror for the underbellies of cars.
Or is it that I'm scared of the sky?

What more welcome to the world
can I muster? What tense do I use to say
I do? This just-past-noon
winter day when you are away
& otherwise undecided
about the clouds in a panic
& the sun
barely lit.

Colonic

A falcon comes in flight to rest on my shoulder.
To a dear sister, it sings, *with love.*
The bombers passing over Guernica swept the stars
into infinitesimal bits of steel—
the fallout soldered into our memory
with the camber of great birds.

In the graveyard the officers proffer hot tea
while here, on the tarmac, the jets come in,
their premeditated beaks
wet with heaven.

The airplanes turn several shades of grey while the country dreams
that dozens of civilizations have risen & fallen here.
Standing in for soldiers, his & hers bathrobes
scatter lavender to lull babies to sleep
& so the babe at the bulkhead yawns a plume of luna moths,
& for a time we are all arrested by our common desire
to explore the rarely traversed places under the stars.

The sand that dazzles your pocket—if you look closer,
it's all you have left of public life.
Yesterday I thought I saw a sugar house filled with small violins.
Yet from my window seat I now see quite clearly— there it is—
a desert,
something so beautiful made of sand.

Revelations

'There comes a time.'
...how the river, running, runs out of itself:
–Pablo Neruda

All of a sudden—the earth shook—
Six black horses emerged from a crack—flames
Hissed & spat as if set by God's fiery taper—
People burned inside their cars trying to escape—

Silver trunks of firs & birches
Watched while we caught our breath—
Every living thing needed shelter—
So we stitched dead leaves into wallpaper
Iridescent as the wasp's nest—

The beauty of the smoking world encircled us—
What could we call it? What could make the trees burst into fruit?—
We roamed among cats, wolves, bisons, ground sloths
& the neighbours' orphan dogs who barked madly—I remember it
Clearly—when the girls ran—their legs pumping—freely
Like their true mammal selves—I could feel some charred filament
In my rib cage light up again—For days we licked each others' faces—
We mourned the last songs of birds—gnats, gnats, everywhere, trapped
In amber—When the girls fled thereafter—their legs sprinting
Faster & their wood spears held mightily in their fists—they
Disappeared for hours—I was the old woman in the woods
From whose hands the horses drank their water—

Pound of Water, Piece of Bread

Tonight the streets turn gelatinous

Dogs trot by with their tongues allol

Hummingbirds scissor the air

Letters shimmer in their liquid

I feel your words against my ear, so large and porous

The ink holds the movement of your hand

Always there's a light coming in by the side door

Always some kiss upon the brow

In my dreams the corridor of coat pegs empties

Whether in this world or that I cannot tell

The tomatoes hang so wholesome in their trance

The past carries its own brand of effulgence

And given the chance to leave the house, nostalgic

Given the sidewalk's propensity to open unto sea

Within a hair's breadth of the city bus, its irascible fender

At the epicentre of bliss is a longing—

My compatriot I wish you were near

Constellation

The first daylight creeps
quietly in

You asleep, and our daughter
tucked into you

as if she lived first
in the cave of your body

Only you've escaped
into her

At the end of her dream
is a kite, a white

kite

flying over us,
over the plum trees,

& their litter of plums out back

It flies over the whole story
of our lives

Of course, it's a dream and so it's hers
and I have only

the bully of my imagination
and love

that no life before this
could prepare me for

Three

To the hills and the mountains under sky

I'm so sorry I hurt you. It's a fresh breeze

They call the rainy season & I've had my head

For too long without light.

There are the salmon, their red

& silver bellies as light leading us.

The grace of elms when you really

Need them.

        Then there is the ocean

So rusted out from its original intention—

Sunlight streams in through the glass

Light that befalls eggs & hatches them

          This particular light eschews performance

Blood, foot, tongue   being

Behold the holy light of the cyclops cast in gold

For faint hearts		for wanderers		for artisans & car salesmen

Ocean is the final resting place

For certain fishes		who store in their organs

Fragments of plastic

To reach someone with special knowledge

We soothe the ocean's bruises

Remember gasoline   our flip-flops idling in the tide?

In the undulating sand & rocks, the light of mica squinting up at us—

Those schools of fish as loose magenta

Streetlights intrude so rudely on lovers touching each other

This is the infamous light that causes blindness

This is an apostasy of light for most prophets

Open ocean, mouth of water, under light—

Is a Corpse. Is Sex. Is an Ovum. Is a Bed.

Serious maternal light makes motion pictures

But no pictures eclipse the beginning of light on Earth

Mothers say Let there be light and There is light

God is illiterate as he can't with his fingers feel it

He meets his dead companion and then offers him plums by the road:

"You wretch, you didn't even hesitate

To gorge yourself on guests in your own home."

In the shiny-hearted territories of spring

With its mad puddles and horny blossoms

Freeway lights adored by writers and drivers alike

Alight again—

Almost as if we hadn't seen them—

So many road signs night travellers abide by because they are shy

Shy about sex and its excesses but nonetheless

                                                                they drive

Somewhere on this hellacious freeway slick cocks gorge in corners

                                                                entirely lit up

Light turns to copper in the park at 5 p.m. and everybody's laughing

When they sing, leaves of light recede

Music like lime Popsicles & bug bites

People pluck banjos and guitars, drink beer in brown bottles

That turn yellow when they hold them up to the sun

Bicycles going full-throttle   fall over at the spectacle of trees

College kids in bobby socks collect goose feathers in cupped hands

Lite-Brite and buttons of light for eyes

They read aloud the queen's remedies by lamp light

Climb to mountaintops where they collect postage stamps and purses

Waddle home & lick their honeycomb fingers

Trailing bonbons & books by Barthes & Bhabha behind them

Stage lights light up the nativity

Mainly for Mister Jesus and his non-equestrian horses

Snowstorms embrace lights and so do their drivers

Also farmers   This is why the hearth is the heart of the home

This is why mammals travel together   tethered by strings of lights

This is why Mister Jesus' mother Mary was a virgin

Whose father kept her in a hole beneath their family home

And waited for the call from Lord Guardian of the Hymens

Before she would see any light at all

Which is the light that ties us?   Which light do we thrive by?

Two bodies splayed on white sheets

Find a tree

Through their fingers—

They lie eating primroses

Dionysus watches them from the Tree of Heaven

With binoculars pressed to his eyebrows

His scalp smells of coconuts

In his hand he cradles a lover's underthing

& sniffs its

Fortuitous light falls only when the chaperones are sleeping

The jubilant light of the mind RADIANT HUMANE BRIGHTNESS

Prozac lights up the minds of the Americas at night

When we should be dreaming

Light illumines the tears of the people weeping they are weeping

(when humans call out · to light

it cannot hear them—)

Hunters of light gather in packs to scavenge vast distances

Together they navigate the woods by the whites of their eyes

We spend our lives—all of us—

Under the spell of voices

Like the Bodhisattva on Hastings

Who sells oranges and cigarettes

"They're coming," he says

"With their curses   their spit

Walk backward slowly   play dead

Whatever you do, don't fuck with them,

Don't talk back—"

My friends, my sweet barbarians,

Epilogue

Somebody dangles from the ninth-storey balcony

Somebody passes a virus hole to hole

The light obfuscates   It coalesces   It recounts

The city battles to preserve a visionary's picture

Watch the girl's once-fruitful mouth decompose

It's not her fault, somebody poured a packet of Pop Rocks in her mouth

See the cops? Across the street reading the newspaper

While the evangelical takes out a comb to grease his hair back

While the mouldy pages of *Popular Mechanics* emit their smell

Somebody's bent over, getting a revolver up the ass

Somebody's authorized not to stare   to keep on walking

To join the national consensus

What she does with all those light bulbs, I'll never know

That one's been awake for seven nights and counting

Come morning, his shot-up face was an open sunflower for the kids

Dropped off at school

Don't condescend to me, honey—

It stops the pain the constant physical pain, she says, and swigs her soda

The cravings will be with us forever, don't you know

Somebody's in the washroom being shaved, lights off

Somebody's shuttling a line of centipedes down a sinkhole

Four

Firstborn

You live in me. We're eating well.
The sky softens into a pulp.
I dream of lampposts,
soft fruit.

When you sleep, you sleep
inside a white city
covered in ash. Streets
electric with silver,
broken teeth.

Soon little fire
you will live here:
lights and sirens,
sky trains, automatic banks.

Soon you will live here.
Come screeching into the trouble.
Come already haunted.

Midwinter

Morning, everything's covered in frost.
Your small body sluffing
its way into the light, sleepy &

trembling like a monster with a beefy heart.

Crows pillage the garbage for pig feet
& artichokes, roam
overgrown, in the chicken scraps

at the same stems of grass. You bat
at the dirty glass &
yell *Get up* to the scrum of them

at the red bicycle—

when one plump mother greets you
at the kitchen window,
                    menaces,

like the dark mouth of the oven
fattening the morning bread.

Flood

Angels wear black. Everybody knows that.
Flies use their feet for building.

When time comes to get the job done
they turn to each other, the fly

& the angel, their faces warped
by lightning & sand.

The angel carries clouds on her shoulders.
At night she wrings them of water

& washes her hair. The fly doesn't bathe—
he's too quick for rain.

But he builds magnificent cities.
Everybody envies his gardens & walls.

The angel sits in the branches of the willow
after days of making sunshine

to suck on a cigarette & sing silly
songs for the street children.

Both of them would like to live a slower life.
But the work is endless, one body after another

needs her hair washed,
needs his bones buried,

a stone rolled over the grave.

Evacuation Procedures

Detonate the hearts of babes

the smart hearts of babes

detonate the hearts of cellphones

of tungsten—

detonate the apartments, carports, bridges

the birds above the marshes

detonate the lovers in their beds

their coffee cups in the early hours

detonate subways & railways & shopping carts

the land mass, land rovers, the monster

traffic jams

detonate the religious paraphernalia

parapets, pomegranates

the watershed the snap dragons

detonate the host and parasite

the beehive the enclaves

detonate the throat in hand

the highlands the Alka-Seltzer

the wunderkind and the wanderer

the small hoods of strangers

the tea spout and the tongue scraper

the spake and the ramshackle

detonate the populous, the popular calculus

& all other humanized processions

Red

As for me, I live my life in red.
–Paul Verlaine

The coreopsis inhabits the corpse.
Grows in the colon like good bacteria:

obedient and needy. Pulses up
toward the sun, prods the esophagus

wanting in. Wanting to become
the resplendent bouquet

of the mouth. Crumbled bone
feeds dirt with its calcium.

Copses of apple trees frame the yard.
Worms circle eye sockets

feeding on lashes and fat.
Buds grow hard through the ears.

Shoot through ducts where tears
once bloomed. Fall falls soon

on the orphan body grown
cold in the garden. Clouds

repudiate the fury of rain.
In the busted shed out back

cats howl. Raptors circle
at every yard.

Red doesn't bother the children

They embrace its sex

These ghost-soldiers march in rows

After the chilled & gruelling hours of midnight

& hoarfrost, frostbite—

Auditioning for the march of the wood soldiers

To sweep the bodies off the roads

To man the manholes and their explosives

To relinquish the shrapnel from the earth

To then replenish it

How many days has red manifested in panic
in pills that spark spells, hallucinations
of green porpoises and antelopes gnawing at stars?
Would you fill my ear again with cyanide, Madam?
Villages drenched in a thousand locusts.
I have told you solemnly, God said—
but red was fruitful and it multiplied.
And so we have Ford factories and assembly lines
where bolts flow into copper swamps,
where traffic jams quiver & collect tires
for fire-eaters with silver tongues.
Colour of nightsky: where are you looking?
Colour of anus: red.

Birds will forever live
in red and never redeem themselves.
No need to. They lie awake in their nests,
creating. Forgetting. Creating.
Wooling their graves, posing,
mostly keeping the sky free
of uranium. Such a pleasure
to view the world through binoculars.
Look at all the birds with bits of red:
cardinals, wattlebirds, summer tanagers
Bohemian waxwings, barn swallows,
rufous hummingbirds and the Memphis Redbirds—
baseball team, by the way, *and* bird.
Birds and their bits of red are endless.

They walk wearing petticoats

while sipping tea. Oolong. Lapsang

souchong. Hatpins hold their hats in place,

corsets contain their porcelain frames.

They promenade arrested by geese—

geese, geese, geese, flying everywhere in flocks—

skidding fast on the face of the lake water.

People as delicate as butterflies, hand-sewn.

A pastoral as bright as the facades of banks.

Trees, bushes and cattails—

sink into the foreground. Meanwhile,

birders wearing wire-rimmed spectacles

fix their eyes on the singular sight

of the red-winged blackbird

                    taking flight—

Transmission towers flash red

Sky interrupted by lightning, by fighter jets

The puffed cheeks of the blowfish

Wheelbarrows and Lay's potato chips

Stacks of plastic coins at Sunday poker

In the hooked spines of the burdock

A red bird becomes entangled

A landmine excises a leg

The perimeter shushes

Gooseberries sit plump

In the thorny bush

Red of long-throated poppies

Red slippers for the weavers outside their doors

Bangles clinking against each other

on the wrists of the women at the market

Herd of mountain goats

slices the river's ruddy current while

greedy honey bees honeymoon

in the blood blossom

Thou art happiest in red

Red music of lies and phantoms

In the red twilight of a quiet house

Stars nailed to an evening sky

Red ramp of dreams

Beyond the profundities of water

Red nest of stars

A nest is a lamp lit with red

A bat flapped from an old eyelid

Into pools of red earth   Yes

Even the brain of the pomegranate—

Red of your open mouth

Red of your midnight hissing

Your half-thoughts, your leaning in

The low sounds of night-calls

Passing through me

Pouring into the dark

The Looking Glass

The wolves ran on through the evergreen forests
–W.H. Auden

At night wolves roam the park
to eat beneath the glass eye of the moon.
Every pleasure stings a little.
Lice and feathers stuck in the mouth.
Sometimes we shit bricks.
Sometimes we lose our speech.
People pay to have their lips sewn shut.
If our guts were filled with butterflies
we'd open our mouths and they'd flutter out—
Mariposa. Papillon. Butter-wing.
Who can neglect
such a fancy list of cravings? O
brumal moon watching over us,
hover at this neighbourhood
staked by stop signs and witness the gusto
of pale red. "Soldiers are coming. We smell death."
We roam in and out of the hedges.
We follow all signs of scattered light,
the blackish-bluish sky lit by silver
cartoons—each twinkling thing
a thing to keep alive. It's
Christmas. Bells jing-a-ling from house
to house. Fog's thick up to the neck and over, cold,
cold, cold, cold, cold, warmer—

Starry Heavens

For this dream we need binoculars.
The sea is fallow and feral. This strange wave
we are now so universally swept up in
is called Chance. Draws us in, draws us out
& under the sea. Griffons peer at us with gold eyes
& mermaids think deeply of the common good.
Through the eyepiece, we spot a horse with wheat in her teeth.
Today this means all action is mercenary.
On land, in sky, the crows fly in murders
to rest on the spines of sycamores. Grey daylight
flattens every landscape & the crows cry tears of ice.
This is Demeter's bonehand so, shake it.
Her touch could mean famine or feast.
People call her Winter because they carry heavy heads—
often the diagnosis is Vertigo or impotence. Philosophers
dip their ducats in wine & stain their teeth. Teeth, what would
language do without you? What of speech? We came home
from the ocean and went to sleep. We felt compelled
to take our clothes off & languish quiet as felines.
This weather devils us midwinter. So we look up
at the clouds to curse, the stars to name them,
to genuflect. For this dream we need
binoculars. Look: Persephone's finger
lights the stars one by one.

Twilight

Toddlers tumble down the winding staircase
into the dark guts of the house. They wear
slippered pyjamas. They share fealties.
Some stash posies in their fists.
It's black. Sour breath. Sour breath.
Rain falls for three days straight but the toddlers
put an end to it—some call them sorcerers,
the way they piss mistakenly and soak it up.
They leave washcloths that smell of turpentine,
pluck the branches off the pink magnolias
to hang their laundry. Inside their mouths
you can count every tooth and stains from tar. Everything
smells like ammonium, the night sky, the mist.
At night I lie awake. At night I press my nose
up against their salty heads. To kiss their meaty
cheeks forever. To never let them go. Toddlers
stand motionless in uniforms. Their badges shine
like stars. They radio to each other, asking, *Is it clear*
now? *Is there enough light to go out on deck*? Some say,
Roger. Some say, *Over and out*. Lightning storms
cackle outside. Maybe hail, you never know. Toddlers
turn cartwheels in the parlour, toddlers
eat mint cakes and tourtière. They can't yet
write letters to their grandmothers, but they
record each other—they say they wish the trees
could whisper, they say the Earth is a square.
They say, *Night-night* and, *Hello*. When the sky falls
as predicted, everybody runs for it, everybody
belts it out for the last go, everyone
except the toddlers—they pitter-patter, they hold
hands, they walk round and round in circles singing ever so
softly, turning and turning, *Ashes, ashes*—

Notes and Acknowledgements

The epigraph from Virgil comes from his *Eclogues*.

"Tenement Song" is for Goran Basaric, Ljiljana Biukovic and Philip Basaric.

"Firstborn" was written on September 13, 2001 with Rory in mind.

Bountiful, BC is a polygamist colony run by Mormon fundamentalists in the Creston Valley of southeastern British Columbia.

"Evacuation Procedures" borrows its title from a yellow safety card handed out to graduate teachers at the University of Arizona English department after a man walked into the College of Nursing on October 28, 2002, and shot two professors as they were invigilating an exam.

"Apiary of Underclothes" is for Brad Cran.

The "Neighbourhood" sequence is for Nadia Thibault, Kevin Paetkau, Sebastian and Deuphine; Tony, Julie, John and Sophie Balantes; Walt and Sally-Anne Haug; Susan Halcrow, Colin Redfern, Maddy and Malcolm; Jacques, Charlotte and Melodie Bodolec and all other inhabitants of Trout Lake.

The poem "Starry Heavens" owes its thinking to this passage from Immanuel Kant: "Two things fill the mind with ever new and increasing admiration and awe, the oftener and more steadily we reflect on them, the starry heavens above and the moral law within."

The graveyard mentioned in "Colonic" is the Airplane Graveyard–Bone Yard at Davis Monthan Airforce Base just outside of Tucson in the Sonora Desert.

"Birds Fly High Here" is for Stephanie Keon.

The epigraph that begins the poem "The Looking Glass" comes from Auden's poem "In Memory of W.B. Yeats."

The epigraph for the poem "Revelations" comes from Pablo Neruda's poem "There's No Forgetting (Sonata)."

Italicized lines on page 52 were taken directly from Homer's *Odyssey*. Here Odysseus addresses the Cyclops in Book Nine.

The italicized line on page 57 comes from Alice's Notley's poem "World's Bliss."

The italicized line on page 61 comes from Gwendolyn MacEwen's "Breakfast for Barbarians."

"Epilogue" is for Clyde Wright, Teresa Chenery, Helen Hill, Bandit, Russ and Jo, Delores Dallas, Tom Quirk and Rosalynn Humberstone, and in memory of Al Tardiff and Tristan Vox.

I wouldn't be here without the grit and steely determination of my grandmothers, Patricia Alice Donovan Brady and Marjorie Ann Dillon Jerome. I thank them both for what they made, remembered and passed on to us all. I also thank my grandfathers Cecil Arthur Brady and James Edward Jerome.

Thanks to my parents John Jerome and Colleen Kerr, my brothers, Paddy Jerome and Brendan Jerome, and Linda and Bruce Cran, for their wholehearted support.

I offer fervent gratitude to Gail Brown and Frances Sjoberg for inviting me to stay at the University of Arizona Poetry Center guest house to work on this book.

Suzanne Buffam and Elise Partridge made this book better. Thanks to Silas White and everyone at Nightwood Editions. Thanks to Ray Hsu, Travis Mason, Matt Rader, Mark Grenon, Kevin McNeilly, Mary Schendlinger, Stephen Osborne and Adam Chiles for reading this manuscript at various stages.

Thanks to the *Colorado Review, Grain, Event, Malahat Review, Canadian Literature* and *Geist* for publishing poems in this book. This book wouldn't have been written without grants from the Canada Council for the Arts and the BC Arts Council.

Thanks to all my teachers, friends and family, especially Brad, Rory and Micah-Sophia.

Gillian Jerome's first non-fiction book, *Hope in Shadows: Stories and Photographs from Vancouver's Downtown Eastside*, won the 2009 City of Vancouver Book Award and was shortlisted for a BC Book Prize. She teaches literature at UBC and her poetry has been anthologized in *Breathing Fire 2: Canada's New Poets*. She lives in East Vancouver with her family.